HR APPROVED

WAYS TO WRITE FUNNY MEMOS

HARMONY HR PRESS

CONTENT

ABOUT THIS BOOK 5

CHAPTER 1: Cleanliness and Organization 7

CHAPTER 2: Attire and Dress Code 15

CHAPTER 3: Punctuality and Attendance 19

CHAPTER 4: Time Management.. 25

CHAPTER 5: Meetings 33

CHAPTER 6: Communication (Email, Casual Conversations, and Noise) 39

CHAPTER 7: Video Calls and Remote Work 49

CHAPTER 8: Team and Staff Motivation 55

CHAPTER 9: Tips, Reminders, and "Unsolicited" Good Intentions ... 63

CHAPTER 10: Use of Office Equipment............................. 71

CHAPTER 11: Last-Minute Solutions and Emergency Calls............... 77

CHAPTER 12: From Subordinates to Bosses 83

APPENDIX: Memorandum Templates (Downloadable) 91

ABOUT THIS BOOK

Have you ever wanted to tell a coworker what you really think, like: "No offense, but you're an idiot"? Or your boss: "Take it down a notch; there are only 24 hours in a day." Or even your subordinates: "If you've got time to chat, you've got time to work." All without risking your job, damaging relationships, or feeling bad about saying it.

If you're reading this book, chances are the answer is Yes.

Expressing what we truly think—whether as a boss, colleague, subordinate, or simply as a fellow human—can be challenging. People's defense mechanisms are often easily set off, and it doesn't take a jerk to do so. Even the most well-intentioned and tactful comments can be misunderstood, sparking tension, straining relationships, and, in the worst-case scenario, getting you fired.

This book offers 75 clever and hilarious alternatives for articulating your thoughts in a way that's fun, lighthearted, and direct. Inside, you'll discover phrases and formulas designed to help you communicate effectively without sounding rude, overly critical, or—most importantly—a jerk. It tackles a wide range of workplace scenarios and challenges we all encounter on a daily basis.

So, whether you're a manager who needs to address tardiness, a coworker wishing others would lower their voices so you can focus, or someone who simply wants their borrowed pen back, this book is for you.

To make it even more practical, Appendix A includes a link or QR code for downloading three customizable memo templates. This feature allows you to hand over a memo that delivers exactly the message you need. The process is simple: choose the appropriate memo, download the template, personalize it with the recipient's name or team, sign it, stamp it, and deliver it.

We believe that before turning to drastic measures, addressing issues with a touch of sarcastic or ironic humor can effectively convey your message while also sparking a few laughs from the team.

In short, this memo book serves two highly practical purposes, both infused with humor: first, as a lighthearted way to hand out a "memo" to someone or a team—for instance, those who let paperwork pile up on their desks; and second, as a subtly serious tool for addressing concerns, such as a department failing to adhere to the company dress code.

Note: At the start of each chapter, you'll find a humorous memo example presented in a structured format. This helps you visualize exactly how the memo would look if you chose to print and formally deliver it. Not only will you have access to clever phrases, but you'll also see how to package them into a polished, ready-to-use memorandum.

CHAPTER 1

Cleanliness and Organization

For lovers of culinary archaeology

Real Memo:

"To all employees: Please remember to keep your workstations clean and make sure no food is left on desks at the end of the day. Thank you for your cooperation."

Humorous Memo:

"Dear team, just a friendly reminder that your workstations are neither museums nor culinary exhibitions. If we continue finding sandwiches from last year or fossilized coffee, we may have to take drastic action... like asking someone to eat them. Thanks for keeping things 'clean'!"

MEMORANDUM

To: Administration Team
From: Office Management
Date: 06/12/2024
Subject: Reminder for Cleaning Workstations

Dear Team,

Just a friendly reminder that your workstations are neither museums nor culinary exhibitions. If we continue finding sandwiches from last year or fossilized coffee, we may have to take drastic action... like asking someone to eat them.

Thanks for keeping things 'clean'!

Morgan Maxwell
Office Management

For the avid collectors of forgotten mugs

Real Memo:

"To all employees: A friendly reminder to take your cups and glasses with you at the end of the day. Any items left in the common area will be thrown away—no exceptions. Thank you for helping keep the space tidy!"

Humorous Memo:

"Dear team, if you've ever misplaced a mug in the common area, exciting news: it might still be waiting to be rediscovered (along with a fossilized layer of coffee inside). We kindly invite you to rescue your beloved mugs before the cleaning crew decides to give them a permanent home... in the trash. Thank you for your cooperation!"

For the creatives who see the world as their canvas

Real Memo:

"This is a reminder to all employees to respect shared workspaces and refrain from using areas like walls or desks for unauthorized artistic expressions. We appreciate your cooperation in maintaining a professional environment."

Humorous Memo:

"Dear marketing team, your creativity truly knows no bounds, and we love that about you! That said, let's remember the office walls aren't part of the canvas. While we appreciate your artistic enthusiasm, the cleaning crew has kindly asked that we stick to paper for our masterpieces. Thanks for keeping your creativity flowing—and our walls spotless!"

For the fans of towering paper mountains

Real Memo:

"This is a reminder to all employees to organize their documents and avoid unnecessary piles of paper at their workstations. Keeping the office tidy helps maintain an efficient work environment. Thank you for your cooperation!"

Humorous Memo:

"Dear team, we get it—there's something oddly satisfying about building 'paper mountains' on your desks. But unless we're planning to start an office Everest expedition, it might be time to clear the peaks. Let's work together to keep our desks less adventurous. Thanks for helping us reduce the altitude of our paper landscapes!"

For the champions of extreme reuse

Real Memo:

"We'd like to remind everyone of the importance of keeping kitchen utensils and shared items clean. Properly washing your mugs and personal containers helps maintain a hygienic environment for everyone. Thank you for your cooperation in keeping our common areas tidy and in top-notch condition!"

Humorous Memo:

"We know you're a true champion of the environment, and your dedication to reusing the same coffee mug without washing it is proof of that. An admirable eco-friendly effort (though maybe a little soap wouldn't hurt). Thanks for reminding us that sustainability can truly stand the test of time!"

CHAPTER 2

Attire and Dress Code

For the enthusiasts of 'extreme casual'

Real Memo:

"This is a reminder that the office dress code requires professional and appropriate attire for the workplace. We appreciate your cooperation in maintaining a presentation that reflects company standards and adheres to established appearance guidelines."

Humorous Memo:

"Your 'totally chill' style reminds us that life is meant to be enjoyed, but unfortunately, we're not on vacation here. While the 'beach mode' vibe is definitely charming, we'd much rather see it in vacation photos than in the boardroom. Thanks for bringing the energy—just without the summer wardrobe to match!"

MEMORANDUM

To: Carlos Belmonte
From: Office Management
Date: 06/12/2024
Subject: 'Beach Mode' Is Only for Vacations!

Dear Carlos,

Your 'totally chill' style reminds us that life is meant to be enjoyed, but unfortunately, we're not on vacation here. While the 'beach mode' vibe is definitely charming, we'd much rather see it in vacation photos than in the boardroom.

Thanks for bringing the energy—just without the summer wardrobe to match!

Morgan Maxwell
Office Management

For those who confuse the office with a red carpet

Real Memo:

"We kindly ask that you adhere to the professional dress code rather than opting for formal or black-tie attire, as the office calls for a look that aligns with a workplace setting. We appreciate your cooperation in helping everyone maintain an appearance suitable for the environment."

Humorous Memo:

"We're truly impressed by your red-carpet-worthy outfits—you've definitely mastered the art of glamour. But remember, the office doesn't have to feel like an awards show every day. Thanks for reminding us we can shine bright without the black-tie attire!"

CHAPTER 3

Punctuality and Attendance

For those who like to reinvent the work schedule

Real Memo:

"This is a friendly reminder that our start time is 9:00 a.m. Punctuality isn't optional—it's essential for maintaining team productivity. We appreciate your commitment to being on time and helping us keep things running smoothly!"

Humorous Memo:

"Hey team, we know some of you operate on a time zone that's... uniquely your own. But here at the office, we like to stick to something a bit more predictable—like regular business hours. Let's aim to show up before our calendars start collecting dust. Thanks for keeping us all running on real-world time!"

MEMORANDUM

To: Finance Team
From: Finance Manager
Date: 06/12/2024
Subject: Let's Travel Together in the Same Time!

Dear Team,

We know some of you operate on a time zone that's... uniquely your own. But here at the office, we like to stick to something a bit more predictable—like regular business hours. Let's aim to show up before our calendars start collecting dust.

Thanks for keeping us all running on real-world time!

Morgan Maxwell
Finance Manager

For the fans of making a 'fashionably late' entrance

Real Memo:

"Just a friendly reminder: punctuality is key to kicking off our workday efficiently. Being on time helps set the tone for a successful day and keeps the whole team running smoothly. Thanks for making it a priority!"

Humorous Memo:

"Team, we all love making an entrance, but let's save the 'late-but-make-it-fashion' vibes for after-work events. Around here, showing up on time helps us all get started on the right foot. Let's make punctuality our new office trend—coffee tastes better when you're not rushing to catch up!"

For those who see punctuality as a distant goal

Real Memo:

"We'd like to remind you that punctuality is a key aspect of maintaining team productivity and efficiency. Arriving on time not only helps you better organize your own tasks but also ensures smoother coordination with your colleagues. Thank you for helping us start the workday in sync and with the time needed to deliver quality results."

Humorous Memo:

"We know punctuality is one of your personal goals, and we have full confidence you'll achieve it... someday. In the meantime, any effort to arrive before the fiscal year ends would be greatly appreciated. Here's hoping the clock is always in your favor!"

For the 'long-break marathoners'

Real Memo:

"Just a reminder: breaks should be kept within the designated time. We appreciate your punctuality in returning, as it helps maintain a smooth and efficient workflow. Thanks for your cooperation!"

Humorous Memo:

"Dear team, we get it—breaks can sometimes feel like a weekend marathon. But remember, they're meant to be quick sprints, not a long-distance race! We appreciate you making it back to the finish line (a.k.a. your desks) on time to keep the flow going. Thanks for staying on pace!"

CHAPTER 4

Time Management

For the Break Time Enthusiasts

Real Memo:

"We recognize the importance of taking breaks for both well-being and performance. However, it's crucial to balance these moments with the urgent demands of work. We kindly ask that breaks stay within the designated time to ensure the workflow remains uninterrupted. Your commitment to responsible time management is essential to the team's success."

Humorous Memo:

"We appreciate your unwavering dedication to break time—it's clear you're the MVP of sticking to your schedule, even when those urgent reports are calling. Prioritizing wellness is important, of course, but maybe we can balance it out a bit? Let's give those reports some love, too. Thanks for keeping both productivity and wellness in the game!"

MEMORANDUM

To: Carlos Belmonte
From: Office Management
Date: 06/12/2024
Subject: Exemplary Dedication to Breaks... and Reports!

Dear Carlos,

We appreciate your unwavering dedication to break time—
it's clear you're the MVP of sticking to your schedule, even
when those urgent reports are calling. Prioritizing wellness is
important, of course, but maybe we can balance it out a bit?
Let's give those reports some love, too.

Thanks for keeping both productivity and wellness in the
game!

Morgan Maxwell
Office Management

For the Masters of 'Tomorrow is Another Day'

Real Memo:

"This is a reminder that meeting deadlines is critical to maintaining the quality of work and supporting the entire team. Delays can disrupt workflows and affect overall outcomes. Please ensure that tasks are prioritized and managed effectively to meet the expectations and responsibilities associated with your role. We appreciate your commitment to keeping things on track."

Humorous Memo:

"Your confidence in 'there's always tomorrow' is truly inspiring. It's a refreshing reminder to take things one step at a time—until the deadline knocks on the door, of course. We appreciate your calm approach, even if it means we'll all be pulling a sprint at the eleventh hour. Thanks for keeping us grounded in the moment... and slightly anxious about the clock!"

For the Overachievers Who Forgot About 'No

Real Memo:

"We want to thank you for your willingness to take on new tasks and your dedication to the team. That said, we'd like to remind you that balancing your workload is essential to avoid burnout. Your enthusiasm is deeply appreciated, but your long-term well-being is just as important to us. Please don't hesitate to prioritize and manage your time in a way that allows you to fulfill your responsibilities efficiently."

Humorous Memo:

"Your ability to take on extra tasks is truly impressive. We're starting to wonder if you've ever been introduced to the word 'no.' While we don't doubt your enthusiasm, we suspect you might need a break... or three. Let's not get to the point where you have to delegate the art of resting, too!"

For the Champions of Slow and Steady Email Reading

Real Memo:

"This is a friendly reminder that checking your email daily is essential for effective team communication. Prompt responses are key to making quick decisions and ensuring that important information is available when needed. We appreciate your attention to this practice to help avoid misunderstandings or delays in the workflow."

Humorous Memo:

"We truly admire your patience and determination in reading every email with absolute calm... even if it's days after it lands in your inbox. You've shown us that urgency is a matter of perspective, and in your case, important information can wait. We just hope that when it's something urgent, your 'here and now' kicks in a little sooner!"

For the Masters of Last-Minute Email Surprises

Real Memo:

"We kindly request that important messages and information be shared in advance to avoid disruptions and allow for organized planning. While we understand that unexpected situations can arise, your collaboration in anticipating these communications is essential for maintaining a smooth and efficient workflow."

Humorous Memo:

"We truly appreciate your dedication to those last-minute emails—especially when we're all just about to head out. You always keep us on our toes, making sure we never let our guard down... not even at the end of the day. Thanks for keeping our adrenaline pumping right up to the final minute!"

For the Calendar-Challenged Report Submitters

Real Memo:

"It has come to our attention that some reports are not being submitted by their scheduled due dates, which affects the team's overall planning. Moving forward, we kindly ask that all reports be submitted on time as agreed. This will help ensure better coordination and a smoother workflow. Thank you for your cooperation in this matter."

Humorous Memo:

"Breaking news: The reports department would love to receive submissions on their scheduled due dates. It seems your reports might have some unresolved issues with calendars. Any chance you could help them make peace?"

CHAPTER 5

Meetings

For the Masters of Marathon Meetings

Real Memo:

> "We'd like to remind you to schedule meetings based on the time truly needed for each topic, ensuring discussions remain focused and efficient. This helps maintain a steady workflow and maximizes the use of our workday. Thank you for your collaboration in planning effective and timely meetings."

Humorous Memo:

> *"Your talent for scheduling meetings is truly impressive. While we're certain not all of them needed to turn into a three-hour symposium, we do appreciate the reminder of the value of patience—and your enthusiasm for exploring every detail... and every subdetail too."*

MEMORANDUM

To: Carlos Belmonte
From: Office Management
Date: 06/12/2024
Subject: Efficient Meetings: When Less is More

Dear Carlos,

Your talent for scheduling meetings is truly impressive. While we're certain not all of them needed to turn into a three-hour symposium, we do appreciate the reminder of the value of patience—and your enthusiasm for exploring every detail… and every subdetail too.

Morgan Maxwell
Office Management

For the Guardians of Endless Conversations

Real Memo:

"We appreciate your active participation in meetings. Your ideas and feedback add value to the conversation and support team decision-making. However, we'd like to remind you of the importance of allowing space for everyone to share their thoughts and contribute within the allotted time. Thank you for helping make our meetings productive and inclusive."

Humorous Memo:

"Thank you for your valuable verbal contributions in every meeting. Without your input, we might experience moments of silence—which, in some ways, could be refreshing. Still, we admire your ability to keep the discussion alive, often with observations that spark deep reflection— or, on occasion, a collective sigh."

For the Champions of Meeting Memory Lane

Real Memo:

"We appreciate your commitment to keeping relevant topics at the forefront during meetings, as continuity is key to advancing our projects. However, we'd like to remind you that reviewing topics once is usually sufficient to ensure everyone is aligned. Your collaboration in focusing on new points will help make our meetings more efficient."

Humorous Memo:

"We truly admire your ability to remind us of everything discussed in previous meetings. Your dedication to revisiting every detail—sometimes multiple times—is truly unmatched. With you around, forgetting isn't an option... and neither is moving on too quickly!"

CHAPTER 6

Communication (Email, Casual Conversations, and Noise)

For the Authors of Email Epics

Real Memo:

"We'd like to remind you that clarity and brevity are key to effective email communication. Keeping messages concise and focused on essential points ensures they are read and understood quickly. We appreciate your effort to streamline emails to support efficient communication."

Humorous Memo:

"We truly admire your ability to turn every email into a mini-series. We get it—details matter! But after each 500-word message, it starts to feel like we're signing up for a new chapter every time. We appreciate your thoroughness, but we also love a good cliffhanger in the form of a quick summary!"

MEMORANDUM

To: Kale Smith
From: Your friend, Jhon
Date: 06/12/2024
Subject: Express Messages

Dear Kale,

We truly admire your ability to turn every email into a mini-series. We get it—details matter! But after each 500-word message, it starts to feel like we're signing up for a new chapter every time.

We appreciate your thoroughness, but we also love a good cliffhanger in the form of a quick summary!

Jhon
Friend

For the Masters of Cryptic Subject Lines

Real Memo:

"We'd like to remind you of the importance of using clear and specific subject lines in emails to make it easier to locate and organize information. A well-crafted subject line helps recipients quickly identify the content and urgency of the message. Thank you for your collaboration in enhancing communication clarity."

Humorous Memo:

"We love how you make every email subject feel like a mystery novel. You keep us guessing, piecing together clues to figure out what the message is really about. While it's fun to solve the puzzle, a little sneak peek every now and then would be a welcome twist. Thanks for keeping us on our toes with every click!"

For the Curators of Email Archaeology

Real Memo:

"To keep our communication organized and efficient, we recommend starting fresh emails instead of forwarding old threads—especially if the previous content isn't relevant to the current topic. This approach makes it easier for everyone to find the right information without unnecessary backtracking. Thanks for helping us maintain clear and streamlined communication!"

Humorous Memo:

"Thank you for taking us on a nostalgic journey with every forwarded email. Opening a six-month-old thread feels like piecing together a historical mystery, complete with endless 're: re: re: re' clues. While we do appreciate the trip down memory lane, a crisp, straightforward email would be a refreshing change every now and then. Don't worry—we promise we won't forget the good old days!"

For the Champions of Office Acoustics

Real Memo:

"We'd like to remind everyone that during periods of high focus, it's important to keep noise levels low to avoid disrupting your colleagues. Loud conversations can be a distraction for those working on complex tasks. Thank you for helping us maintain an environment that supports concentration and productivity."

Humorous Memo:

"Your voice brings energy to every corner—it's impossible not to hear you! You certainly keep us alert and engaged… though sometimes, a 'volume down' button wouldn't hurt. Thanks for keeping us informed, even when we're trying to stay focused!"

For the Masters of Uninvited Insights

Real Memo:

"To maintain productivity, it's important to keep workplace conversations focused on topics that support project progress. Non-work-related discussions can disrupt the team's workflow, so we kindly ask that contributions remain aligned with relevant tasks. Thank you for your collaboration in fostering a focused and efficient environment."

Humorous Memo:

"We admire how you manage to join every office conversation, even those you're technically not part of. We appreciate your concern for the collective well-being... though some details might be better saved for those directly involved. Thanks for keeping the spirit of inclusivity alive in every chat!"

For the Philosophers of Inopportune Timing

Real Memo:

"Respecting each team member's time is essential to maintaining a productive and considerate work environment. While informal conversations are welcome, it's equally important to ensure everyone has the space to manage their time according to their priorities. We value your willingness to share your thoughts and kindly ask for moderation to allow everyone to focus on their responsibilities."

Humorous Memo:

"Your talent for sparking deep conversations at the most critical moments is truly one of a kind. You get us pondering the mysteries of the universe... just as we're trying to focus on a major project. Thanks for adding a touch of depth to the most unexpected moments!"

For the Masters of the Monday Interrogation

Real Memo:

> "We appreciate your friendly attitude and genuine interest in your colleagues' well-being. Courtesy and communication are essential to fostering a positive work environment. However, we'd like to remind you that while personal interactions are always welcome, it's important to respect each team member's time and personal boundaries."

Humorous Memo:

> *"We've got to admire your curiosity—you ask about our weekends with more detail than we can even remember! Thanks to you, every Monday feels like a friendly interrogation—if only to confirm just how uneventful our lives really are."*

CHAPTER 7

Video Calls and Remote Work

For the Virtual Meeting Virtuosos

Real Memo:

We kindly request that video calls be scheduled in a way that does not hinder daily productivity. Scheduling unnecessary meetings or holding them at inappropriate times impacts team performance and adds unnecessary strain to the workday. We ask that you prioritize addressing essential matters without relying excessively on constant video calls.

Humorous Memo:

"You're a true pro at virtual meetings—we've mastered every expression you make on-screen. That said, we sometimes miss those rare moments of quiet where we can, you know... actually get things done. Thanks for ensuring we never go without a video call!"

MEMORANDUM

To: Kale Smith
From: Office Management
Date: 06/12/2024
Subject: Always Connected, but with Breaks

Dear Kale,

You're a true pro at virtual meetings—we've mastered every expression you make on-screen. That said, we sometimes miss those rare moments of quiet where we can, you know... actually get things done.

Thanks for ensuring we never go without a video call!

Jhon
Office Management

For the Experts in Flexible Remote Work

Real Memo:

"We'd like to remind you of the importance of maintaining a suitable work environment while working remotely, ensuring that virtual meetings are conducted in a space conducive to focus. Effective organization of your time and workspace supports project progress and promotes clear communication. We appreciate your collaboration in optimizing performance during remote work."

Humorous Memo:

"We truly admire your approach to remote work and your unique sense of 'time management.' Balancing calls, the couch, and the fridge is no small feat. You've inspired us to discover new strategic spots for virtual meetings… and to always keep the fridge within arm's reach, just in case."

For the Masters of Convenient Connection Issues

Real Memo:

"We'd like to remind you of the importance of maintaining a stable internet connection during virtual meetings, especially during key discussions. Consistent participation is essential to ensuring the flow and success of our meetings. We appreciate your cooperation in ensuring a reliable connection to avoid unnecessary interruptions and keep projects running smoothly."

Humorous Memo:

"We know you have a real talent for making your connection mysteriously 'drop' right when meetings heat up. Your ability to vanish at the perfect moment rivals that of a professional magician! One day, you'll have to teach us how you make the internet 'go down' exactly when it matters most."

For the Experts in Remote Work Mystique

Real Memo:

"We'd like to remind you that keeping your camera on during video calls is essential for effective and professional communication. Lack of visibility can impact the dynamics and focus of the meeting, so we kindly request that you actively and visibly participate in each session."

Humorous Memo:

"We've come to admire your gift for turning every meeting into a game of hide-and-seek. Are you quietly listening, multitasking, or just a figment of our imagination? One day, we'd love to see you on camera—just to prove you're not the Loch Ness monster of remote work."

CHAPTER 8

Team and Staff Motivation

For the Green Thumbs and File Whisperers

Real Memo:

"We'd like to remind you that organizing and regularly maintaining work files is essential to ensuring an efficient and orderly workflow. Keeping information updated and in good condition makes accessing and using documents easier when needed. We appreciate your dedication to giving your files the same attention and care you apply to other tasks in your workspace."

Humorous Memo:

"Congratulations on being the only person on the team who's managed to keep a plant alive for more than two weeks. It hasn't gone unnoticed. Maybe you could teach the rest of us how to care for plants... and possibly our files too?"

MEMORANDUM

To: Kale Smith
From: Office Management
Date: 06/12/2024
Subject: Master of Plants (and Files?)

Dear Kale,

Congratulations on being the only person on the team who's managed to keep a plant alive for more than two weeks. It hasn't gone unnoticed.

Maybe you could teach the rest of us how to care for plants... and possibly our files too?

Jhon
Office Management

For the Caffeine-Fueled Motivators

Real Memo:

"We'd like to remind everyone that enthusiasm and mutual support are essential for maintaining a positive team atmosphere. We appreciate your efforts to motivate others and foster an environment where everyone feels valued. Your contribution is vital to the team's collective success."

Humorous Memo:

"You've got an incredible talent for energizing the team—particularly when coffee is within reach. Whether it's rallying us with 'Almost Friday!' or just being a constant source of positivity, you're basically the caffeine we didn't know we needed. Thanks for keeping the office vibe alive!"

For the Eternal Optimists of the Office

Real Memo:

"A positive attitude goes a long way in tackling daily challenges and inspiring the team to perform at their best. Your uplifting energy is truly appreciated and makes a meaningful difference in the workplace. Thank you for helping create a more productive and enjoyable environment each day."

Humorous Memo:

"We truly appreciate your unshakable optimism, especially when you assure us that 'it'll all work itself out.' With you around, even the toughest challenges feel manageable... until we inevitably circle back to them. Thanks for being our resident beacon of hope!"

For the Unsung Heroes of Teamwork

Real Memo:

"We truly appreciate your willingness to support your colleagues when they need it. Your readiness to share knowledge and collaborate in challenging situations strengthens teamwork and fosters a sense of trust. Thank you for being a reliable source of support for others and contributing to the collective success of the team."

Humorous Memo:

"You're the team's go-to lifesaver, always there to pull us out of the quicksand when things get messy. If the office had a 'panic button,' your name would be engraved on it. Thanks for always saving the day—and for not demanding snacks as payment for your heroics!"

For the Standard-Bearers of Excellence

Real Memo:

"We recognize and deeply value your dedication to maintaining a high standard of performance in your work. Your commitment to quality and precision makes a significant impact on every project and serves as a positive example for the team. Thank you for your continued efforts to achieve excellence and exceed expectations."

Humorous Memo:

"Your productivity is on another level—do you have a secret formula, or are you spiking your coffee with something magical? At this pace, we're convinced you've got superpowers you haven't told the rest of us about. Thanks for reminding us every day that we're just a few (dozen) cups of coffee away from catching up to you"

CHAPTER 9

Tips, Reminders, and "Unsolicited"
Good Intentions

For the Policy Innovators with Big Ideas

Real Memo:

"We'd like to remind you that any suggestions for improving company policies should be formally submitted through the established communication channels. We appreciate your enthusiasm and dedication to proposing changes, but we kindly ask that these recommendations be presented in a structured manner for proper consideration. Thank you for following the established process."

Humorous Memo:

"We always appreciate your creative take on improving company policies. It's like planting seeds for the future—maybe one day, one of them will grow into an actual policy. Then again… maybe we'll just keep admiring the seeds."

MEMORANDUM

To: Kale Smith
From: Office Management
Date: 06/12/2024
Subject: Maybe Someday!

Dear Kale,

We always appreciate your creative take on improving company policies. It's like planting seeds for the future— maybe one day, one of them will grow into an actual policy. Then again… maybe we'll just keep admiring the seeds.

Jhon
Office Management

For the Wellness Advocates Among Us

Real Memo:

"We'd like to remind you that each employee is responsible for their own wellness habits, including staying hydrated. While we appreciate your enthusiasm for promoting health, we kindly ask that you limit reminders and personal recommendations to avoid unnecessary distractions for the team."

Humorous Memo:

"Your commitment to hydration awareness is unmatched. With your perfectly timed reminders, we could never forget the reusable bottle staring at us from the desk. Rest assured, we're sipping our two liters a day—if only to dodge the next hydration alert. Thanks for keeping the office flood-free!"

For the Culinary Enthusiasts of the Office

Real Memo:

"We'd like to remind you that respecting others' dietary preferences is essential to fostering an inclusive and harmonious work environment. While we appreciate your enthusiasm for sharing wellness options, we kindly ask that personal dietary recommendations be reserved for moments when colleagues actively seek them. Thank you for understanding and respecting individual boundaries and preferences."

Humorous Memo:

"Your excitement for all things leafy, green, and sprinkled with seeds is truly contagious. While we're still mastering the art of pronouncing 'quinoa,' we genuinely appreciate your wellness tips… even if our hearts (and stomachs) remain loyal to pizza."

For the Advocates of Well-Intentioned Advice

Real Memo:

"We'd like to remind you that maintaining a respectful work environment includes being mindful of each team member's opinions and preferences. While suggestions for improving organization and well-being are always welcome, we kindly ask that you respect your colleagues' personal boundaries and moderate unsolicited recommendations."

Humorous Memo:

"We admire your dedication to improving our lives, one unsolicited tip at a time. Whether it's reorganizing the pantry or trying meditation, you always have a suggestion ready. You've almost convinced us that one day we might actually try one... almost."

For the Keepers of Lessons Past

Real Memo:

"Having a record of past projects is essential, but we encourage focusing reviews on key takeaways. Constantly revisiting the specifics of past mistakes can hinder the team's progress and divert attention from current objectives. We kindly ask that feedback be limited to what's strictly necessary to ensure the team remains forward-focused and goal-oriented."

Humorous Memo:

"Your ability to recall every detail of past projects is truly unmatched. You recall every success (and every misstep) as if it happened yesterday. With you, no mistake is ever forgotten—or forgiven. Thanks for keeping every little detail alive and well!"

CHAPTER 10

Use of Office Equipment

For Fans of Infinite Paper

Real Memo:

"We kindly remind you to use paper in the office efficiently and responsibly. Printing multi-page documents or making excessive copies indiscriminately impacts both the equipment and company resources. We appreciate your cooperation in reducing unnecessary paper consumption and optimizing printer use."

Humorous Memo:

"We admire your passion for paper. Every time we hear the printer running nonstop, it feels like we're in the middle of a bustling newsroom. We truly appreciate your enthusiasm—though we're pretty sure the printer (and maybe a couple of trees) wouldn't mind catching a breather now and then."

MEMORANDUM

To: Administration Team
From: Office Management
Date: 06/12/2024
Subject: Less Paper, More Trees

Dear Team,

We admire your passion for paper. Every time we hear the printer running nonstop, it feels like we're in the middle of a bustling newsroom.

We truly appreciate your enthusiasm—though we're pretty sure the printer (and maybe a couple of trees) wouldn't mind catching a breather now and then.

Morgan Maxwell
Office Management

For the Masters of Vanishing Pens

Real Memo:

"We kindly remind you that office supplies, such as pens and other stationery items, are shared resources and should be used responsibly. We appreciate your cooperation in ensuring these materials remain available for all team members."

Humorous Memo:

"We're in awe of your ability to make pens vanish—it's like watching a magic act in real time. At this point, we're wondering if we're funding an underground pen museum. But no worries—if any pens decide to return from their 'vacation,' we'll keep their little adventure a secret. No questions asked!"

For Keyboard Snack Enthusiasts

Real Memo:

"We kindly remind you that consuming food at your desk should be done in a way that doesn't impact the cleanliness of the workspace or shared equipment. We appreciate your cooperation in maintaining a tidy and clean environment."

Humorous Memo:

"We admire your dedication to multitasking, but your keyboard is starting to look like a snack bar with a secret menu. Every key seems to hide its own little treat. While we're truly impressed by your ability to snack and type, maybe let's keep the snacks on the plate instead of between the keys. Your keyboard—and IT support—will thank you!"

CHAPTER 11

Last-Minute Solutions and Emergency Calls

Fans of the Last-Minute Plot Twist

Real Memo:

"We'd like to remind you of the importance of managing tasks and organizing time to avoid end-of-day emergencies. While we understand that unforeseen issues can arise, we greatly appreciate your collaboration in identifying potential challenges early on to maintain an efficient and organized work environment. Your efforts in this area are key to the team's success."

Humorous Memo:

"Your last-minute emergency calls right before clock-out are always a delightful twist to the day. The thrill of a 'quick fix' at the eleventh hour adds just the right amount of chaos—sorry, adventure—that the team will surely cherish tomorrow. Thanks for making every day's finish a story worth sharing!"

MEMORANDUM

To: Kale Smith
From: Administration Team
Date: 06/12/2024
Subject: Last-Minute Emergencies… Right on Time

Dear Boss,

Your last-minute emergency calls right before clock-out are always a delightful twist to the day. The thrill of a 'quick fix' at the eleventh hour adds just the right amount of chaos—sorry, adventure—that the team will surely cherish tomorrow.

Thanks for making every day's finish a story worth sharing!

Administration Team

For Creators of Last-Minute Magic

Real Memo:

"We greatly appreciate your creativity in problem-solving and your willingness to find solutions when unexpected challenges arise. At the same time, we kindly remind you that planning ahead and anticipating potential difficulties can help reduce last-minute pressure and result in higher-quality work. Your collaboration in timely task management is highly valued."

Humorous Memo:

"We're impressed by your ability to pull off creative solutions right at the buzzer. That said, starting a bit earlier might make the magic even more dazzling. Thanks for proving that creativity doesn't rush—except when it absolutely has to."

For Night Owls of Creativity

Real Memo:

"We appreciate your commitment and dedication to the work, especially when tasks arise outside regular hours. However, we kindly remind you that effective planning helps reduce the need for extended hours, allowing for a healthier balance for everyone. Your efforts to manage priorities within the established timeframe are greatly valued."

Humorous Memo:

"Your gift for spotting urgent tasks after hours is nothing short of inspiring. Who needs a clock-out time when the best ideas seem to arrive precisely as everyone powers down? Thanks for proving that creativity doesn't sleep—it just waits until we're about to leave."

For Masters of the Last-Minute Twist

Real Memo:

"We kindly remind you of the importance of managing projects in a way that avoids last-minute emergencies. While we understand that some situations are unforeseen and appreciate your willingness to address them, effective planning helps minimize disruptions and ensures everyone can stick to their schedule. Your efforts to anticipate potential issues are greatly valued by the team."

Humorous Memo:

"We really appreciate your talent for last-minute 'emergencies' right before clock-out. The timing is impeccable—just when we thought the day was done, you bring the plot twist. Thanks for making every exit feel like the thrilling finale of a suspense movie!"

CHAPTER 12

From Subordinates to Bosses

For Delegation Wizards

Real Memo:

"Clear delegation and coordination of tasks are essential for the team to progress effectively on projects. Proper organization and precise distribution of responsibilities at each phase are critical to achieving our goals. Your collaboration in maintaining this order is indispensable and greatly appreciated."

Humorous Memo:

"We truly admire your almost magical skill for delegation. One moment it's your task, and the next, it's everyone else's problem— like clockwork. It's impressive how you manage to unite the team while keeping yourself 'occupied elsewhere.' Your presence is always... spiritually with us."

MEMORANDUM

To: Kale Smith
From: Administration Team
Date: 06/12/2024
Subject: Magical Leadership: Everyone in Action… Except You!

Dear Boss,

"We truly admire your almost magical skill for delegation. One moment it's your task, and the next, it's everyone else's problem—like clockwork.

It's impressive how you manage to unite the team while keeping yourself 'occupied elsewhere.' Your presence is always... spiritually with us."

Administration Team

For Fans of the 'Urgent' Action Movie

Real Memo:

"We kindly remind you that the 'urgent' label should be reserved for truly critical situations requiring immediate attention. When every request is marked as urgent, it becomes challenging to prioritize and respond effectively. We appreciate your collaboration in clearly identifying priorities to help the team manage time more efficiently."

Humorous Memo:

"'Urgent' might be your favorite word, boss, and every email from you feels like the start of a high-stakes action movie. At this point, we're practically certified in emergency response. That said, if you ever decide something can wait until after morning coffee, we promise the world won't explode (and neither will we)!"

For Masters of Elastic Hours

Real Memo:

"The current deadlines for certain projects are proving difficult to meet. I'm fully committed to giving my best effort, but I would greatly appreciate considering a possible extension to maintain the expected quality. Any adjustments would be incredibly helpful."

Humorous Memo:

"It seems my hours have become wonderfully elastic. However, I regret to inform you that I've yet to crack the secret of extending a day past 24 hours. Perhaps we could collaborate on adjusting deadlines to better fit within the confines of basic physics?"

For The Celebrities of Focus

Real Memo:

"Frequent interruptions are making it tough to maintain focus on ongoing projects. Maybe we could set up a structured follow-up schedule to streamline the workflow. Your support in making the most of our time would be greatly appreciated."

Humorous Memo:

"My focus is so in demand, it's practically a celebrity. Maybe we could set up a schedule for interruptions, so my productivity gets a chance to recover from all the fame. Much appreciated!"

SHARE YOUR THOUGHTS!

Thank you for joining me in this unique collection of memos. If any of them made you laugh, reminded you of someone, or were helpful to you, leaving a brief review would greatly encourage others to discover it too!

APPENDIX

Memorandum Templates (Downloadable)

This appendix offers a variety of memorandum templates tailored to the situations outlined in the book. All templates are available for download and can be easily edited, allowing you to customize them to fit your specific needs.

How to Download

To get the memorandum templates, simply scan the QR code below. You'll be taken to a page where you can select and download the templates in an editable format.

Note Be sure to personalize each memo with the appropriate name or team before printing. Remember, well-placed humor can be a powerful tool for effective and respectful communication.

Made in United States
Orlando, FL
13 December 2024